THE
INTERPRETATION
OF A BLACK LIFE.

By

Zamiyah Ben-Israel

D1445490

First paperback edition May 2020

ISBN 979-8-6464-0372-9 (paperback)

ISBN 978-1-4767-4660-9 (eBook)

Library of Congress Control Number: 2020909082

3

Table of Contents

4

5

7

SECTION 1: Poems Based on Systemic Oppression

Audacity

With American stripes
embedded in our backs

from welts of red to the
flesh's of white

we are outcasts.

With the recipes of mammy

now in the hands of sanders

along with the molasses of
Jemima

we are bamboozled.

When the attraction of our
livelihood became wearable,
that is when we were
mimicked,

9

but still, we rise into cabins
of despair

And into the gospels of
Stockholm.

How ironic that we ONCE
were.

Stocks, bonded and sold on to
Wall Street where our foot
stones still lie to this day,

Left with no compensation.

Strange Fruit

Uncanny is the apple as it
falls from the tree

How can I enjoy the fruits of
my labor when they are
strange to me?

Peculiar I may be

For thinking of such

But if I'm not mistaken

America's love for us

was never that much

And America's pie is

Rather shy

With all the barriers they
posses

11

But still, we try to find ways
around it such like a quest

Not noting the sweet
potatoes, we finesse

Is the best

As I digress, Strange fruits of
our labor Were never in our
favor

So, our demise is like

The candy

Either

Now or later.

Those that Stayed
Inside

Are you my professor or my
oppressor?

Already I see strife within
you.

What is it?

My looks?

My attire?

My attitude?

As a matter of fact, I don't
care

I paid for your teachings.

For the obvious reasons

Not being this.

13

Why are you so proud?

Bring your nose down

And loosen up a little

They don't care about you

So, stop showing off.

I ask the question

not wanting a response.

Are you my professor or my
oppressor?

You look just like me.

But then again, they did have
black overseers.

To Be Black

To be black Is to be

Prominent.

To be "black" is to be

Chosen.

But to be black in America

is to be targeted

and sometimes Helpless.

Race to Melanin

They say the organ matching
system is colorblind
Yet ours are the only ones
being reached for
All the time.
Guilty by association
Or is it
Death by pigmentation?
When is it a good day to be
black?
That day seems to be
indefinite
What are we?
Black donors or
black **C**ommodities?
Black market, our organs are
what sparked it.

Worth more than titanium,
gold, diamonds, and crystals.
What's the issue?
Maybe it's our cell tissues
tested in the labs where
Henrietta's once lied
Died from police stops and
gun pops
Puzzled and jig-sawed
Suns best friend and man's
best profit
Bodies sold down the same
roads of the silkworm.
Moms and dads have no clue
or no option
But stare at the tears
and
scars of their offspring.
Brown parts in the veins
and appetites of state senates

17

And on the asses
and backs of rich bigots.

What Am I?

In darkness eyes and teeth is
all you can see of me

When I arrive, they hide

Streets are crossed

Hats on beds

Walks under ladders

And purses on floors

They would rather, then, for
me to tread their way.

Perceptions are made

Way before I could greet

So, my self-esteem is at the
same level as my feet

What Am I? A Black Cat or a

19

Black Man?

A Black Woman's Misconception

I used to say at least I'm not a
black man

And forgive my ignorance or
maybe I was naive

But for some reason, I
thought

That we had some trick up
our sleeve

When it came down to
protection

Or

Should I say

Exemption.

I guess it was my perception
of us

Being the muses of their
fetish

Or seen as a non-threatening

Factor

But

What became dreadful

is that I was wrong.

Sisters are being killed from

Left to right

Every day, every night

Every hour, every second

With every weapon

Every road rage, every police
stop

Every provoked argument

I guess I didn't do my
research

Or maybe I chose to neglect
it.

I know what they did

In the past to us

Why would I ever think

There would be

Any sacrifices

Due to lust,

As a black woman

I don't get a pass

I am as much of a threat

like my brother

I once thought to be nothing
like.

Rest in peace Nia Wilson

In the Waters of Flint

In the waters of Flint

Lies a host of parasitic
officials

That has infiltrated the soils
of the people

And by the soils

I mean their bodies.

Ambushed by Poisons of lead

and

abused by the tortures of
waste

The aroma is a mixture of
deception and despair, and
the taste is of negligence.

It's quite frank who's to
blame

In the depths of their voices,
no shame in their game

For now, will not the people
of Flint have to worry about
lead from the officer's pistol,
nor will they have to worry
about the lead that's not
being used in

*their children's pencils....no the lead
that's in their pipes*

Will do just fine.

SECTION 2: Poems Based on Stockholm Syndrome

The New Jim Crow

The new Jim Crow

Is what the colored soil

Sow's

As it continues to flourish,
the awareness

Of our demise does not grow

Yet the opportunity of
incompetence

proudly show

Because times have changed

And

The way things once were,
are no longer the same

29

Overtaking failure is much
easy

And conquering victory is
much stronger

The fate of our black men

Is gambled with

As we hold on to them by a
thread

Shrunken shoulders

Bows of head

And

Hopelessness is what they
shed

Voices are kept shut

While pockets are weighed
heavy

So, they die on their knees as
oppose to their feet.

It is noted that America's
oppression has sprung
amongst the black race,
specifically the black man,
because he is the foundation.

4th of July
Flashing Lights

Sparks fly as they cheer

While freedom was in our
eyes

Freedom wasn't in their
minds

But still, we salute and watch
flashing lights

Can't distinguish the
difference between gunshots
and fireworks.

A celebration that was never
intended for thy 3/5's for
those freed were still
doomed.

With Strange fruits of their
labor

July fourth was never in their
favor

So, they hide under their beds

So, they can hopefully evade

The dangling of their heads

And the hanging of their
necks

Bangled bodies toast on tree
post

and torn hearts of the little
ones,

On all American postcards.

I wonder why we still
celebrate Independence Day.

Mammy and Me

Mammy and I Is all I see She
loves and cares for me

Yet distrust and hate her kind

I don't mind

Our relationship is more than
fine.

She raised me better than my
mommy, her incompetence is
precious, and her holy ghost
antics make me laugh

But she gets angry when her
kinfolk

Say the word cracker.

34

she yells the same word my
father says to her

"NIGGER"

she attacks them with sticks
and rocks until she sees welts
and knots

Mammy screams at her
kinfolk all the time

Mammy must really dislike
them

Mammy must really like
crackers

That explains why she's so
fat.

All Black A'int Gold

How should we feel?

About the Ojay's and Freddie
greys?

As they say, they don't want
any black babies

Especially for those like Luke
Cage and Taye Diggs.

They have a problem with
our wigs yet praise the

Extensions and contoured
frames of the same ones that

can't be us.

You know the copycats.

If you ask them,

they're fine living the life
with their trophy wife

No such thing as Emmett Till

That is until things go south

And their pockets caught a
drought

Or even worst

The same black bitches are
carrying their hearse.

Do we protest? Do we put
our lives on the line?

But if we don't

To the media

We'll be

Bitter Bitches.

Validation

They feel as if

It's not valid unless the
masses

have it.

We Wouldn't dare buy black

But will support corporations

That funded our plight

As the salts of the earth

We provide flavor

to everything.

So why must we continue

to seek

validation?

From those that mock us

and steal our gifts
and monetize from it.

SECTION 3: Poems Based on Invasion of Privacy

Cotton Comes to Harlem...

But no this is not the cotton,
to be blossomed or picked

Nor is this cotton to be worn

Bought or sold

This cotton's use is to
infiltrate the soils of a
domain it does not own.

To bare all malice

It arrives and observes as it
absorbs

All its delusions it began to
spread its confusion. An
epidemic that quickly
captures the minds of the
dwellers

42

Exploit and alter traditional
habits while at the same time,
introducing new ones.

It destroys, rebuilds

Then wonders why?
What does this do to the
natives? Well it entirely
outcasts them from their
community, leaving them
with no alternative but to
leave.

Placebo OF THE
NEGRO

As I walk amongst them, the
suspension isn't what they
possess

For they are to be consumed
with propagandas and MK-
Ultras, we've perpetuated.

As I trick them with the
illusions of inclusion,

I break unity.

When I trek down their
avenues, lost, I am not.

For they think I'm accepting
them, but I'm appropriating
them.

When I take pictures, I am
scoping.

When my uncanny stares
alarm you,

I am planning

I marginalize their success to
1%

And make sure Jewels aren't
dropped along the way.

Takedown pro-truth leaders

And manipulate them to
mirror my views.

Accuse them of self-afflicted
systemic issues

Take their women,

45

Soften their men,

Confuse their children and
protest their rights to life.

Them becomes all,

Theirs becomes ours, and
why? Becomes, why not?

Yet they still love us,
Stockholm goes a long way
for sure.

Next Stop South

Ole cotton has come to the
south

and has caused worries and
wonders

Across thine mouths

With rigorous amounts of
luggage

and

Restaurants bought, and
black souls sold

HBCUs have folded

With the tip of their hats

and welcome mats

We've already seen what
went down up north

That that was once green has
run its course

Southern bells aren't ringing

Nor are

Church choirs singing.

But ancestors are rolling
over.

Sulfur brings

Mammy and sambo

and as far for Uncle Tom
goes well, he never hides

Cotton causes bulging eyes

Firm struts

With shucks and jives

Charleston blue is posted
outside.

Ole collard greens and

smothered chops

are packaged and

stamped to the docks,

Where they will be

bought and sold

Under a new name…

and that is gentrified

Vanity Interlude

Vanity's thoughts

Is of vain.

As she flaunts

From the spoils of rotten is
what she strains

Surrounded by mirrors on her
wall

She sits tall

With backaches

Vanity cracks

Walls break...Humpty now
she Is

While her Lips, teeth, and tip
of the bum

50

Was rearranged

She contours her flaws to 50
shades of spray

For vanity, it's insanity.

By trying to elude her
situation-yet, she can't escape
her reality

So, she glues the prosthetics
of her idol

Ebony.

The body that can't be
mirrored.

For vanity, it isn't fair

As she pouts-she shouts

Why not should I have to
care

51

Nor will I dare to step out
with a crinkle or a tear

for thy name is vanity

And I am here.

She piles make-up for hours

and her contour techniques
made her climb the social
ladder.

Showering Compliments

and glistening gifts Isn't
enough

as they dine, she wines

"Humor me," she says to the
mirror, and now her exterior
is no longer tough.

With an ego as high as the
very mountain

she once sat on

competition is rough

she falls

and stalls

for help

To whom can she call?

She masters the art of war

as the days began to fall
yearning for elasticity is what
she adores.

53

Those very same crinkles and
tears began to appear on her
skin, as she cracks and sags

Vanity nags.

The fruits and enemas can't
shake what's in her

and that is recessive.

Section 4: Poems based on Family Dysfunction

An Athletes Wasted
Potential

A pair of carties,

fresh T, some suede loafers

and off to the parties.

Yes, with an S

Which includes sex, and the
whole nine

Even though that's less than
what he has in his pocket

But he's a scholar

or at least he could have been

that is if he didn't drop-out,

but fly guy happens to be an
expert at finesse.

As he arrives at Homecoming

He shows off to the
freshman's

hoping their impressed,

but when the game starts

He happens to see his old self

On the field

and is now depressed.

When Patriarch Flee

I battle with myself literally

Surrounded by estrogen

Not enough testosterone in
the house

So, I do what's best to
balance it out.

I flee as you did

Into the streets

Trying to find a source of
direction

But it's like I'm dyslexic
because I can't seem to focus
while school is in session.

I bully, I fight, I steal

Not because it's within me

But

That's how I feel.

I'm Too Young to be a man

Why you left me with your
shoe and pants size?

I'm not ready to walk in them

Hell, I can't even fit them

And from the looks of it,
neither were you.

I didn't ask to be here

From what mom's told me

You wanted me here

So be here

Matter fact, don't

Beware.

I'm bigger, and I'm stronger

And angrier now

More harm than good

Is what you will do

As for a clue, I have none.

Yet abandoned by you, I was
raised by my mother and for
that

Will, not my seed, face the
jettison feeling I had as your
son?

Testimony of a Black Woman

No bending knees

My integrity will not flee

Here I stay grounded, with
my crown tilted

But still on me

There I will leave
because dysfunction

I will not spawn.

…

For one day, the crown will
be passed down to my
daughter.

Worry Wart
Fallacy of face

Maybe I think too much

After all, I've seen

to many matriarchs caved in

And I refuse to be a carbon
copy of "waiting to exhale"
or "the Diary of a Mad Black
Woman."

They say, not to worry, and
"the right one will come one
day."

And maybe that's true

It's not like I'm looking right
now, but I am curious

The way this generation is
setup

I'm too much of a gem

To just let anyone in

Of course, my focus is on my
career, but sometimes I think

Will my success be too
intimidating?

Already they are intimidated
by me

I'm poised and with my grace

I am radiant

A true phenomenon.

I silent rooms and turn heads

But I am no trophy

and refuse to be treated as
such

I guess time will tell until
then I will pretend not to
worry.

To Catch a Black Butterfly

You must seek out

At its caterpillar stage

when it's less jagged and
more persuasive Not yet wild
but

like a butterfly, she's sharp
and more engaging

vibrant like sound

Soft like silk

And graceful

A moving shadow without a
host

Rarely seen as if it was a
ghost

Best of its kind

No colors, patterns, or shapes
could hover its shine

Yet it gets weakened

And

Outwitted by flowers-which
that are wild

So, when caught, she reverts
to the ways as a child.

To be its catcher

It's net melts hearts

Synonymous to Fry

He knows her path and guide.

Timid and introverted ways
have now become nothing
but a phase.

To catch a black butterfly is
to ruin its value

But to nurture, a black
butterfly is to gain its glory.

Based on a true story

Says a Black Mother to Her Son

Take what I'm saying to you
now

Please don't wait till I'm
dead to unclog your ears and
lift your head

Why must I wait until then

Tattoos on the chest and your
mind filled with sorrow

That's not what I need

What then suddenly, my
words of wisdom

Will be studied, recited, and
abided

68

Like the rappers, you look up
to

Why not look up to me

I struggle, I strain, I fight, I
break through-with you

Shit for you

I smoke out of stress

That you caused

Look up to me

I know a father is something
that you wanted

But he's not here,

he's not here.

It's About Time

Although time has flown

for me

The position in which I once
stood

Did not

Lost I was

But now, I am awake.

Change

Is now in my range

Why?

So, I won't have to explain to
my seed

The reason Why I have not
flourished

was due to me laying on his
grandmother's couch.

What if a Crip Wore Red?
Would his decision cause

large

amounts of blood to be shed.

Would he then change the C
to a B?

Runaway when trouble
came?

or

Stood ground to fight for his
domain?

Would the blue in his veins
turn against him?

Would his anthem dance
cause gout?

Would the homies leave

While he finally began to
wear his heart on his sleeve?

When he wears white

There's no fight

Ducks or run-ins

Surroundings are of peace

So, No longer must he reach
for his piece

But what about that back-
pocket flag

Something that should be
lagged

What if a Crip wore blue
would he have a clue on what
to do?

Where to move?

73

Who to trust?

When to shoot?

Although he chose white, his
pick was red.

Red all over

His head

And shoulders

Knees

And anything but humble
clothes

He needs a blood transfusion-
they scream

But What about that flag

That lies beneath his clothes

Dashing plights

74

And flashing lights

Of red and blue with white in
the middle

A message too deep for him
to understand

So, the cycle continues.

Section 5: Poems Based on Black Excellence

Mommy and Daddy

She was like a swan

Long, beautiful, and quite

Not like the goose's, I was
used to

See daddy was loose

Kind of like the chickens that
flocked around me.

As they clucked

I ducked

because swan was in my
sight

All I would think of was her
and me

Every day and every night

Although she saw me as a
wolf

That huffed, puffed, and did
damage

For fun,

Little did she Know I would
melt for her

as if she was the sun.

Soon Mommy came to her
senses when I asked her out

as she saw that I was as
serious as she was.

Longevity weighed on me
heavy

For one day

I knew she would be my
wife.

Silk at its Atypical State

Being black is already a
fashion statement
It's a commodity that's too
exotic for emulation.
Yet it is always attempted.
With its fine threads it
Draws attention
Blacks have risen from being
Ignored to adored
was synonymous to dirt, yet
Evolved to expressions and
consultations
Only complications are that
they are free agents
That can't seem to find any
representation….

Synonymous to Black

BLACK;

The most hated

With all the envy and anger
perpetuated

BLACK:

The most degraded

With all the bias and
stereotypes syndicated

Not so much celebrated

Yet constantly appropriated

Guess who doesn't appreciate
it

Black.

Not allowed to be frustrated,
and if so

How would you see it?

After all, it is BLACK

Black is also everlasting

Black is everything

Black is everywhere

From the moment

you close your eyes.

To the bold ink, you press

On our paper

Black is beautiful

Black is fly

Black is gold

Black is bold

Black is life

Black is proud.

Rides to Timbuk2

Bumpy

Drivers sometimes grumpy

Music playing with latches
on doors swinging

Torn seats and cushions
exposed

Will the siren pull us over?
Well nobody knows?

Dashing down avenues and
Catching those on the curb

Along the way

Through the window, I can
see how drastic things have
changed

thinking

Will they take that 2

What am I talking about?

You know the cab that was
once a dollar is now 2

Will the vultures take what's
left of This moving culture?

That we so gracefully sit our
buts on

Busses competitors

And

Passengers saving grace

Not that much space, but gets
us from place to place

On-time, and it cost way less
than

a taxi ride

Damn I scream

What are we, patsy?

Household name contrary

to Its fair.

Dollar cab, are you still
there?

1st Gen

Not sure what to do with this
knowledge

Sweat is what lies on my
forehead

With stomps of pressure on
my shoulders

I wish I could dust off

Wonders of what-ifs are
spoken

Worries I pedal

Holding on to my perceptions
of how it will be.

No ladders left

Just roads less traveled

88

No know-how or what to
do's in my circle

Naive support is what they
sport

Passed down Stories of
legacies

Are my heirlooms

And knowing who I am is
what

Strengthens me

Not Riches but wealth and
health

Is what I owe to them

So, there's no need to start
over again

Not sure what to do with all
this knowledge

so, I cry as

I take my first step to college.

State of Befuddlement

I thought

I thought I was in a Brooklyn
state of mind

That was until I returned

I thought I would be fine

I mean I love my city

But what is felt now is the
envy

Almost everything has
changed.

Broke natives and high-
priced shoeboxes

91

Is what I see

The culture

Well, the culture has lost its
touch.

Whether it was sold, stolen,
or naively given away.

The days of our glow Lays in
an ashtray.

We are now surrounded by

Marlboro cigarettes, art
obscurity, middle-class
stoners

and "quote-on-quote
philanthropist".

Our brownstones are no
longer heirlooms

Just considered to be the ones
that got away

Our streets they're neat

But it's not like us

I mean we like graffiti

and legendary portraits

Our music is forbidden.

Nor are props given

When Sally's and Nathan's

Rock our merch

and kick back and sip angry
orchards on our turf

I mean, we have a curfew on
how loud we can be now.

Their dogs' shit is dominant
on our playgrounds

Paradises have crept threw

These ghetto concretes

Yes, they look nice

But the grounds aren't for our
feet.

Whatever we seem to adore

No matter how obscure

Is never ignored by them

They steal what's real

and make it appeal to them.

O Ye Desolate One

They hate to love me yet do it
so well.

How can I tell?

When compliments and
stares shower my way

They stop and glare with rage

Those that do this are
dangerous.

When I light up a room, they
swoon in caucuses of
defense.

Give me strife as a reflection
of their plight.

And

Challenge anyone who sees
my presence as delightful.

Try and try to ostracize

Me to be the odd one, (in fact
maybe I am, I'm such a gem)

I take it in full

When I'm poised

They tend to make lots of
noise.

My taste is acquired

And of scarcity type, theirs
be expendable.

A cut above the rest is what
is seen when looked at me.

They fear what they don't
understand, and attack what

they lack, so I'm what they attack.

Aside from what's known, Being the center of attention isn't always good when people are plotting and scheming on your livelihood.

Although I walk in a room full of snakes, I stand tall, never look down, only to admire my shoes. I adjust my crown, thank God, and strut like no one's around.

It's all a part of the process